a ruckus of awkward stacking

a ruckus of awkward stacking

matt robinson

INSOMNIAC PRESS

Edited by Jill Battson
Copy edited by Jan Barbieri
Designed by Mike O'Connor

Canadian Cataloguing in Publication Data

Robinson, Matt, 1974-
    A ruckus of awkward stacking

Poems.
ISBN 1-895837-86-3

I. Title.

PS8585.O35172R82 2000 C811'.54 C00-932238-8
PR9199.3.R53475R82 2000

The publisher gratefully acknowledges the support of the Canada Council, the Ontario Arts Council and Department of Canadian Heritage through the Book Publishing Industry Development Program.

Printed and bound in Canada

Insomniac Press, 192 Spadina Avenue, Suite 403, Toronto, Ontario, Canada, M5T 2C2
www.insomniacpress.com

For
my family and friends,
especially my mother;
for Marissa

Table of contents

Acknowledgements

Many thanks to the numerous individuals who helped in working these poems to their present states: James Arthur, Michael deBeyer, Jonathan Dewar, John Ford, Mark van Dam, and everyone in English 6123: Poetry Workshop; Ross Leckie, Mark Anthony Jarman, Tony Steele, and Christoph Lorey; the folks at the bi-weekly Friday night workshops in the Ice House; Jill, Mike, and everyone at Insomniac; the UNB English Department and Creative Writing Program; my family (especially Mom, Dad, and Nick); Marissa Allison; and the editors who have expressed an interest in my work.

A number of the poems in this collection have appeared in the following publications and journals: *Aethlon: The Journal of Sports Literature, The Antigonish Review, Bywords, Carleton Arts Review, Contemporary Verse 2, The Cream City Review, The Dalhousie Review, The Danforth Review, Envoi, Event, The Fiddlehead, FreeFall, The Gaspereau Review, Grain, The Harpweaver, Kaleidoscope, Matrix, The Nashwaak Review, The New Brunswick Reader, Other Voices, Pottersfield Portfolio, Prairie Journal, Queen Street Quarterly, QWERTY, Signal, The Wascana Review of Contemporary Poetry and Short Fiction, Whetstone, Westerly, The Windsor Review, Writers' Forum* and *Zygote*. Some poems have been featured on *querte*, the online version of *QWERTY.* Versions of some poems have also been featured on CBC Radio. A selection of poems from this collection won the Writers' Federation of New Brunswick 2000 Annual Literary Competition Poetry Category.

A version of "apostrophe: a mess of floor" won the 1999 Petra Kenney Poetry Prize. A version of "what we sometimes mistake as love: the right hand of a pioneer radiologist, 1932" received 3rd prize in *THIS Magazine's* 2000 Great Canadian Literary Hunt. An earlier version of this collection received Special Honourable Mention in the 2000 Writers' Federation of New Brunswick Alfred G. Bailey Prize Poetry Manuscript Competition.

one

a ruckus of awkward stacking

the language of flowers

when speech fails we learn
to communicate in

a syntax of bloom and
stem-length inflections.

the staged whisper of roses —
heavy, red with prom night
aspirations. the hot bother,
the idle chatter of a greenhouse
floor: all snippets and coloured
interjections.

        amputations piled
and dying together.

a black-eyed susan sentiment.

we speak this
garden tongue

because we know the bloom,
   the going to seed.

landscape architecture

i.

it was a forensic undertaking; a structuring,

an engineering of empty space. and the brick
walkway we built is now a fingerprint of our loss

and recovery. there were, of course, the obvious
constructions: the framing and piecing together;
the bricks and patterns with their metaphors. but

there were the subtleties of sand as well: the layering
of coarse and fine, the burial of the one as a beginning,
a foundation; then the compaction and its resentment

of movement; and the final filling in — the sprinkling
of ash, of silica, and the way it slowly disappears,
falling in, away among the bricks, antiquing them.

it is a dynamic cartography, this clay mapping
of our loss. ours is an engineered, interlocking grief.

ii.

and there is something, i think, in my father
sitting on the edge of the steps, an age of cracked grey
paint sticking to his khakis — trying clumsily,

roughly, to break bricks. to get pieces appropriate
and small and odd enough to fill the awkward
spaces where the new walkway collides with

the old peeling paint foundation and the steps.
hammer in hand — the same ageless implement
from last summer, ten summers ago — he swings

down across the union-made clay face and
punishes the earth for not acknowledging
his plan. at the moment of impact there is

a pause and then an explosion of dried blood dust
and shards as tears of sweat slide off his forehead.

late june

i am dead-heading geraniums.

the initial, boisterous assertions of spring
have become suggestive whispers coughed
under hot breath.

the colourful frenetic has spent itself
like an eager drunken lover. and here,
in the garden centre, the complicated

tangles of roots grow tight
and uneasy and intricate in
their plastics. the parking lot

blacktop is different shades of grey — stained
and crowded like the aftermath
of sex. it dries uneven and patchy — while

i am dead-heading geraniums

and the day is undecided, alternating
between the cool anticipatory
tickle of a skirt-sway breeze and

still heat — oppressive
and final like varnish. my skin is soft
wax, each hair a wick. there are leaves

and clusters of bloom on the pavement.

geranium

the metallic of a geranium does not seem out of place
here, among the sedum and sport-utility vehicles. it is
an olfactory irony, manufactured of earth and linen, all

sterilized, in bags. here, where the chicken-wire
geometry of asphalt pens broncos and mustangs, it is
in keeping with the miracle of a sheep's recollection

of a field, all tidy and bagged, for sale. today there are sods
in a trunk on plastic, and that wonderful parking lot odour,
the metallic of the geranium, swirling in the reflected heat.

notes towards a garden glossary

i. axil

*the corner formed between a leaf or a
branch and a stem*

all taped and bulbous, all bulky with the idea
of support, there is a rush of green. a leaving

home: a ruckus of awkward stacking. and this
turning, this departure, is like a cardboard death

for the one; an engineered end. all dry and faded
brown, there is a possibility of brittleness, of

a break. as for the other: it dreams of indeterminate
things, of the possibility of rain for itself.

ii. runner

a stem growing along the surface of the
ground that often gives rise to new shoots,
roots, or plants

a desperate escape, this
    mining disaster's logic

of tunnels and passages and
connections.   a trench's perverse

    ecosystem: all topsy-turvy life
and burial, death and earth.

iii. thatch

a layer of organic material, between
green grass blades and roots

this is the stuff of the process
of remembering: the dust

on the lp you're trying to play
on your father's circa 60's

rca with the broken needle. it
is the jam on the pages of that

library book. these are the in-between
bits of context and liquor and age

that scratch faces and colours
and names off a list; these are

the mechanics of forgetting,
the active ingredients of loss.

iv. stipling

fine speckling caused by insect feeding

in retrospect, it could be seen as the beginning
of it all; the freckle of a malignancy. it is the way

the sun dances off the face of a watch's wrist
infirmity, and how that reflection of light is set off

by the skin's aging play, its loose brown juxtaposition.
the one creates, while the other illuminates.

the way the markings of a trout are most brilliant as
it struggles with the mechanics of death, flailing

against the spurious buoyancy of science
in the moist light of mid-morning or

afternoon. perhaps there is a longing for a cool fluid
place, and a confusion simply as to how to get there.

v. rhizome

an underground stem

and in culmination, there is this
secretive growth, a development of

something, hidden. a reversal, a movement
backward, underneath — undoing all

the complication until it is reduced
like long division or fractions or something

else that confounds the majority. this is the
algebra; the inequation; the remainder.

cash register view

the fallen blooms and muck deltas are an old skin,
    discarded,
after the asphalt's transformation. and though the
    neutral grey of sky
hangs sluggish, inattentive, it is something more
    than water
that drips, that tears, from the green tangle of
    shards that is
the dracaena in front. from the cash register it is
    the heat of a jungle

become liquid; the perspiration, the fluid kinesis of
    this transformation.
and seen through this tangling of moist emerald,
    the orderly yellow of
the parking grid suggests symbols from the gilded
    language of an as
of yet undiscovered civilization. the alloy glint of
    that hubcap — the sun
betraying an eye while the traffic rustles against
    itself: a mess of leaves.

home again, summer

        the air in my father's guest room,
my old room re-painted, is saturated.
and these sheets cling: wet and sour
like a night-time accident. i am accordingly awake:
aware of my skin's wax-slow melt and
glow; of, among other things, the passage of time.

        so when the startled summer red
of the alarm clock display blooms and smudges
in the heat, it helps me realize the dark humour
of unnatural returns; it takes me across town
— through intersections sluggish with the hour
and the humidity — to where, at a nursery
somewhere, the salvia transplants bake;
a parking lot tattoo, moist and ablaze like a heat rash.

parking lot pastoral

gasoline swirls. beautiful
like bruises, leaked
diesel and un-

leaded lakes irrigate
this asphalt. reclaim it.

an irony like birthday cake:
sweet, layered; too
decadent to

be healthy; ornamental. the
chemistry of the memory

of an animal revenging
ideas of
branches, roots, leaves.

from the ocean, inland

halifax: the afternoon is hot and passengers
gather, a condensation by the departure gate windows.

bags scrape against the tile floor. as the time
approaches, a tide-like order develops. redevelops.

later, in motion, the window is a charcoal or pencil
sketch, smudged; all newsprint concrete and power

pole t's: repetitive and unsteady —
a grade one printing exercise. somewhere

before bathurst we are a drive-by
theatre; we are a travelling circus, mid-way.

an old man, a buick, a mother, two kids: soda pop sticky
with summer, the people stare and wave themselves away.

after coffee, the drummondville morning
is workmanlike; a grass stain on faded denim.

on approach, montreal is a spilt pallet
of cardboard boxes, bleaching in the sun.

two
a sort of lip-read language

still

this cold morning, tangible breath weds fog.
my fingers remember last night's embrace.
the cold, the mist, the hour conspire against
tactile reminiscence. my hands: still, warm.

abstract

        there is nothing abstract
about the human form divine. i think it was
bowering who wrote that. (so i wonder if
he'd never met you.) no picture, chart, or map
proves a definitive route or passage from
the small of your back through the blades and
past shoulders to neck's nape. there is no public
signage, there are no sidewalks; nothing
concrete to take me from lobes to lips. (so,

        perhaps the two of you
have met — some chance encounter, a collision
on a crowded street — and he does know. there
may well be a path he traced, a mapping only
he is privy to. and it could be that this possibility,
this play between my knowing and my not, is
the attraction.) so — explore, survey, enjoy you
as i may — yes, your tongue speaks: but not in
words; and i understand, but not with ears.

morning flight

you left this morning after
the alarm i'd set didn't go off.

i'd asked you last night if i could call and change your ticket,
and you said the idea of marriage scared you some days.

so even though i don't normally get up much before noon
on saturdays, we went downstairs and waited

for your cab. and afterwards, in my room, taking off my sweater
that you'd returned, i fell back into the mess of our bed,

found your sports bra — reached
and breathed you in —

then grabbed my mug and made instant coffee, watching
the microwave timer count down.

katie, christmas, 1900   j.k.b.

    now, in hindsight, it's quite obvious
it was never really mine to begin with;
it was only another temporary situation.
a sort of holding pattern, a cataloguing. and
really, that first signature should have been enough
to let us both know that. that, perhaps,
presents aside, it wasn't — that giving isn't —
always permanent. that things change

hands. and so those first, perhaps, most
interesting, of all the words contained within
are there — inside the cover; in a fine hand,
written. and the cover, too, is a kind of hint:
black, finely tooled and gold-embossed; almost
casket-like for all intents and purposes.
it was a gift from a time when such things
were commonplace. in fact, there are even dead

blooms and other ironies folded between
the pages. but despite all that, it has aged better
than you, than us.   and now i imagine
you, sneezing with the dust; straining
on old, unstable chairs, and reaching for
the book you'd thought i'd like. (at a time when
that mattered — a time when allergies
were just another tingle, a minor inconvenience,

yet still the most troublesome thing
we shared.)   come to think of it, i'm curious
now — curious as to whether or not katie liked

byron either, as to why you were able to
get this, to give this.   and despite
this sudden rumination, i rarely open it anymore,
preferring, instead, to assume things, to
vaguely recall; to let the dust stay settled.

poem; or, 18 lines on desire
      — for m.

        here, on the carpet, i want
to hold you like a new book
of poems: gently and with
the edges of my fingers
tingling — echoing the new and
important lines and their sensations.

        here, in the chair, i want
to taste you subtly — like
the whispered syllables of words
read aloud and alone to yourself at night,
like those of stories finished after
a child has long since fallen asleep.

        here, in the kitchen, i want
to immerse myself in you
as in new dishwater — to cleanse
and sting myself in your acuities;
to run my hands along
unseen liquid edges and discover.

fever

—*for m.*

here, tonight, i can lose
myself in your sickness —

in the incremental warmth of
the various areas of your

back as we lie, together,
here, in the middling part

of the evening. so as my fingers
skitter across your fever, a

thermic memory of our interactions,
i, too, am engulfed by

the freckling blaze, its moist
heat. and your heavy wash of breath

is a sort of chesty crackling
that, in its sounding, becomes

a combination, a consumption, of
it all: this biology, this us.

the morning as continuation
— *for m.*

last night you told me of the moment when, at
    night, walking through
that wooded path — its ripped sweater elbow
    tangle of darkened roots

and branches — on the way back from the movies,
    the two of you were
startled by the instant shadow of a rabbit as it, too,
    returned or left. of how

you reacted by hoarding air (in, perhaps, a confused
    attempt at flight). and
now, later, with the early stitching of our sleep
    barely, and poorly, lit by

the morning sun, i, too, am caught off-guard by the
    brief animal of your finger
as it tracks the crooked direction of my arm. i, too,
    breathe deeply and

embrace the sudden tinge of contact — and,
    understanding all the better
now the idea of instinct, i turn towards this: the
    memory of an incident.

three
scleroderma

spring

the streets tonite are
crystalline; white, and

this cold: harder and
more violent than

second-day-of-spring
march should be. mom is

making funeral
arrangements (but not

to plan ahead). i've
come to realize

people die weather
or not; whether or

not it's rain, sun, or
snow. they go. they go.

dash 8

early black morning with its pink
meniscus dawn. a book

of short stories and the propeller hum
conspire hopefully in a confusion

of sight-lines, of plot-lines; a
complication of this flight to wakefulness,

to a move beyond the uncertainty
of this hanging on the air. and this

vertical syntax: it serves to discount
the peripheral — to ignore

where i am going; to confuse
why i am going, and whether

you'll be there to read this. at sunrise
— landing. a recognition. i see.

another flight
— *after M. Ondaatje's "Flight"*

(though he made no mention of it)
— here it is early morning. and in the pink
half-light: an air nova dc-8. and there is
no seventy-year-old lady, there are no braids,
and although the cabin is half-dark, half-way
between fredericton and halifax, there is
no long white hair. my mother has no hair,

or little. the pins (and tubes) not
in her mouth, but arms. and what with the nurses
and relatives, i wait two hours before reaching
— turning instead to pages, to the seeming
permanence of print; to a woman who leaves
only on my terms, when i am finished; only
when i close my eyes or turn a page.

hospital recliner

there's a cot. they've given us a cot but no one (my father, my
brother, any of us) wants to be the one to take it — to be the most
comfortable as we wait. this is how furniture becomes penance, how
the way a room is laid out is religion — takes on the importance
of purple at easter. the recliner, all hospital vinyl and
crackle, is a fine choice in the middle of the night. so,
too, are the guest chairs: they are to elbows as pews to knees
and low enough to meet the neck at just the spot — wrong
and awkward, like a christmas necktie.

                            but to be catholic is to
dismiss ergonomics in any number of senses: take the kneeling
or the guilt like varnish, dull and ugly, that coats it all. so
in that spirit, it's all the better there's no cable
in the visitors' lounge, that the lobby tim hortons closes at six.

thick with congealed cream

you receded cup by cup, a gradual sipping, your
   slipping away
from us. it began with the ban on coffee. first, just
   upstairs, and
then later, during even my late night brewing
   downstairs in the midst

of chaucer or plath or some other filtration of
   loss, you'd yell or
pound on the floor, your feet still all caffeine-lively,
   it seemed,
and tell me the smell was making you nauseous. i
   wondered

how. how it could make its way up from the
   perk and out of the pot,
swirling around the various corners and up the back
   stairs into the den
where you, all blanket and tubes, all oxygen hum,
   sat absorbing the hours.

it was all about coffee, even the end. i was back
   home from school
having kicked the habit for two months. (a province
   away, it still seemed wrong:
the scent, the dark, the comforting hand-warm.)
   but after a day we'd begun

to head down to the tim's in the lobby, a brief
   respite that had more

to do with leaving than with roasts or presses or
   sugar and cream, or the lure
of caffeine. a sweet release in the worst possible
   sense — i began to sneak

   a cup or two. first, downstairs, barely leaving
   the lobby, then gradually
making my way to the elevator and then to your
   floor, your wing. soon,
i was all the way up to the lounge and then outside
   your room. you

   didn't seem to mind. it was tea for aunts, and
   triple-triples for dad and
a brother along for the trip. i was experimenting,
   with new combinations.
i was home, having a cup and a shower, when dad
   called and said

   we'd better come in. and later, when we returned
   with your things,
there was coffee spilt — a sticky remnant; a residue
   on the phone,
the floor, the table. it was all over and no one
   complained.

at the funeral home

it came as a surprise;
i was suckled on a

mythology. and then
we were ushered downstairs

the day after mom died.
uncles, dad, my brother

and me. then into the
next room for free drinks, snacks.

lack of sleep swirling in
morning; a non-dairy

creamer in our coffee.
expiration dates and

containers: this a new
vocabulary, truth.

new gravestone in winter

and you become concrete, again.
granite-grey, but hazy —
like the stone-dusted labour pains
of this incarnation.

you, again.
a stone.
a name.

between your flesh
and this dust-
ing of snow
(which
   makes this, your winter,
   real)
lies

a name.
a stone.

when, on christmas eve,
these flakes
            fall
around and on us as
we walk
(cold dust upon our
   flesh)

you again become concrete,

(heavy on my flesh,
  heavy as a stone),

completed:
flesh and
dust,
not name alone.

burial

It was not meant to hurt.
It had been made for happy remembering
By people who were still too young
To have learned about memory.

— from "A Short Film" by Ted Hughes

it was not meant to hurt,
as such, that ritual departure. no, it was instead a release:
a place for tears and words and suits; a cause for dressing up —
the ties and cuffs an awkwardness become physical.

it had been made for happy remembering — that black,
that stone, that monument to and of
the earth that you'd become. now physical,
chiselled, and polished: a monochromatic. and so,

by people who were still too young
to think themselves a cargo, (something other than
the mingled sweat and breath of late-night dance and
drinks), you were carried on. a bone weight. and now i know

        to have learned about memory
is to have buried something, to have left it and returned
only to find the object gone and a metaphor remaining;
spring grass as the only colour, the only movement.

kicking away at it

as a child, it was my soccer coach who
let me in on the secret; showed me
the trick to it. standing there, each of

us, with a leg held back and bird-like
hopping, he came up behind me and
simply said: *focus on one thing, one spot*

on the grass. and training my eye to
a piece of clover, i was steadied —
assured. from that point on, through

each of our field-held rituals, i stared:
at bare patches of earth; at longish
blades of grass fortunate or wily enough

to have escaped the mower; at scraps
of paper; and, at times, even at
a shining dime that in the midday

sun would signal to me from just
across the pitch. it was a foolish
sort of looking — we laughed at its

simple efficacy, did not see the use of it
beyond summer's shin-guarded play.
but now, it is early winter, and i am

here in another field, the grass having
slightly wilted, faded in the grip
of frost. and now, as they lower you

down — past the bare pilings of earth
here poorly covered by the green, but
artificial, trappings of ceremony — i find

myself staring at the stones. and
even as i struggle to maintain my balance,
i am slowly moving back: from this

cool october now to the warmer junes
and julys when staring at the scarring
of a field was steadying. then the wind

picks up and sneaks underneath
my collar — and i am back here again,
craning slightly, awkwardly, to find

a spot beyond the crumbling edge of
the hole. i am peering again for that trick,
the secret that will allow me balance,

allow me to stand through this later,
straining ritual; through the sudden
tension and precariousness of my pose.

sea wall, york redoubt

You like it under the trees in autumn,
Because everything is half dead.

  — from "The Motive For Metaphor" by Wallace Stevens

     i like this place now in its muddy
march renewal because it is agreeable — because
in its sopping confusion of footprints i am free
to stumble and not recognize my doing so

     in hindsight. but i also appreciate the
willingness of these remnants of the wars, of those
greater struggles than mine, to align themselves — in the
midst of their own haphazard tumbling

     and collapse — with something akin to
my grief; to allow it something of the concrete. and
the cooperation of the weather, of the harbour's incessant
crashing and its rock-spit, is also a sort of liquid

     kinship. a coupling and mingling that,
while not surprising given the cycles, the multiplicity
of water, is a sympathetic sort of storming. indeed,
that everything here is fully dead, or seems to be —

only the cracked, dark spruce hint at
growth, at life — is helpful too, if only by suggestion,
as, through previous experience, i know that even
this salt-beaten concrete is split by greens in spring.

drifting

from the living room and your worn patch of couch,
    sodium spoils the innocence of snow
        as the plow rumbles by our street
        lamp. as flakes fall all of this is sullied — a
yellow suburban annunciation.

and now as my mug, my egg-shaped mug
    your sister gave me, grows emptier
        (and colder) in my hand, i drink this coffee and
        think of tea, of coronation street silences;
    i remember the afternoons.

so in the yellowgrey of early morning, in the winter-furnace hum,
    i observe the state of water as it dies
        in piles along the street, and in this light
        try to convince myself that the chemistry of
memory is permanent.

minutes pass. snow falls, my shoulders ache in anticipation.
    something in me below the clavicle seems to say it's better
        to let storms blow, let walks disappear.
        that sometimes it's better if we wait it out, if we
don't recall graves.

a comforting archaeology, this

that's the tough part. take the bed,
                the other half,
for instance.

when they take their leave, when
the forms are filled and filed,
when the news ends,
               it begins.

strange, varied —
the things that fill.

a detritus of habits
settles
in the contours of a mattress's
reminiscence:
a crossword-puzzle book and
unwashed sweater sediment.

anything for fill. even
the routine of an alarm clock —
all artificial —
a neon and plastic assurance,
becomes warm and steady like breath.
the ease in reaching it, in turning it off, and
the reality of the excavation — the only
inconveniences.

becoming earth

a memorial, a myth-making: this
victoria day weekend was a mass
of earth. (for the first year everything is
liturgy.)

we looked at what was left:
   baskets. last year's bacopa — a mess
   of hair, lost. (the drugs, you know.)

so we planted —
we were zealots filling
planter after planter:
zinnias, verbena, marigolds — our offerings,
attempts.
we bought more, filling the various spaces.

biblical, we packed the deck
with terracotta;
filled that shady spot in back by the shed
with euonymus because
her chives were alone

in the earth. the colour of
dried blood, it stained
our skin, wedged its way
under nails and behind ears.

then on the tuesday: rain
and driveway rivers — meeting, merging. and
the wednesday it seemed things had been
watered in. settled.

with the beginnings of zinnias' reds, evidence
of a comfort in the ground.

13 ways of looking at fish, after

at another time or place the other dozen might
be more readily available, but for now, cooking alone,
all her kitchen will allow is this

one version. and so i think of fish
as simply the way in which my hands become my mother's —
summer-slick with august, flour,

spices. and all the while there is the sizzling
mimicry of cast iron and butter; a cool
moon fading into the dark

heat. so standing at the counter between
the sink and the stove, i hesitate, refuse to rinse my hands
and instead let the breading

cast and harden. but in the interim
the butter has melted away, and i can reach only for
something transparent and black

at the edge. it is only after the slap and
sizzle of the fillet that i rediscover the butter and notice
the flakes falling away from between my fingers.

october, once removed

there are cigarette butts
on the pavement: bee-frantic, they hive and
gather here in a moist asphalt depression. spent,
even they manage some attempt at animation,
at reincarnation. and you have been dead

for a year. and it seems i've entered that
noisy stage of grief — the kind that creaks and
strains at night in this snap october cold
with the tension of metaphor's gravel that crunches
and sticks to the bottom of a shoe, consciously

underfoot. a year and i had yet to realize
that you had become the rocks, the sea, the mug
my coffee was in, and somehow not dead; less
buried, once removed. i had written you off: a stone
in a field i likened to pencil lead in a lip — poised yet

uneasy. now i'm drinking more coffee;
this year i brought the perk with me. and my holding
the mug, the smooth ceramic, and thinking it a lover —
a liquid knowing washing over me and lapping
gently, like comfort in the folds of sheets and legs —

was wrong. it is a mother, swirling, and
i am a child groping, sleeplessly mumbling; a remembered
foetus swimming through this warmth, this drink.
there is indeed a subtle violence in the way
cream slowly disappears, swallowed into coffee's brown.

picture postcard seagull, peggy's cove
— *after my mother; after a photograph by Mark van Dam*

it is a photograph. and it is what remains
of a seagull after the heady conspiracy that is flight

ceases — ends in a tumult of bone, granite, bone.
and in mailing this picture postcard to my younger brother

on his birthday, i want to convey to him, to let him know, that
even in my absence (perhaps all the more so) i, too, know

something of the suggestive properties of a location, of
a situation. i want my younger brother to know that

even here, in another province, i, too, am learning the intricacie
of our new speech — another language with its fractured

syntax, its bleached bone white and sun-worn hieroglyphics.
and so through this image and its stamped discussion

of some of the finer points of flight, like its conclusion —
solid and unavoidable like the glacial remains

that punctuate this card's bruised ochre paragraph of land —
i hope to make clear the need for us all: my brother, my

father, myself — to listen for and look for the haphazard
scatter of that other feather-thin diction of chance

recollection; thin as the rarified air of peru or some other
mountainous region, somewhere else we have yet to be.

she drank tea

they are nothing
but memory
and memory is short

remember me she says

— from "caught in the sky" by Patrick Friesen

they are nothing —
these small adjustments. and this
switch from coffee to tea:
subtle and unavoidable. — dad's place
has only instant. and
the coffee-maker, now
mine, is a province away, is nothing

but memory.
so this change, this alteration of
my behaviour while home for christmas,
certainly has nothing to do with my mother,
his wife. and my insistence on tea even in the face
of my father's having merely one bag left
(which proves she is now but a memory,

and memory is short —
her decorative tins now ash-sprinkled
at their bottoms as they sit up on her stove)
has nothing to do with grief. this,
as i sip, i am quite sure of. quite sure.
although, later, in the whispered hiss of the kettle,
her kettle, i am sure it is

remember me, she says.
and as the milk swirls and fades, a smoothing
of these sometimes bitter leaves, there is
still a familiar warmth that moves from bone
china through skin to bone. so much so
that i start and the cup trembles, unsure,
while fluid spills over the lip; stains, and stays.

four
like ticker-tape

road trip

what precipitates this early waking, this
preparation for a drive, is death,
among other things. — the funerals
of parents

   of friends, coupled
with my birthday. and despite
the seeming possibility of a correlation
between the two, it is at first
an uneasy suspension, a
mixture that struggles against itself and
refuses any permanent association.

so as the streetlights fade in the wake
of this dawn's sluggish illumination — a dying
tyndall effect of sorts —

i think nothing of it, and

              it is only later — on
the road with everyone else
in the car, with the day's brilliance
having dissolved
the stubborn individualism of those streetlights, having
consumed them— that it occurs
to me.

   and so when someone mentions the drive
as *our first road trip,*
        i squint at the overwhelming

immediacy of the glare, and
turning slightly from the windshield, hope
we don't take anymore,

    not like this.
and at that moment, that instant of everything
outside the car becoming lost in a sudden
wash of sun, i realize that i don't like the end, the
let down, the parting, where you drop
                everyone off;

    that it's hard to drive home
alone. that memories don't hold up
their ends of conversation— they just sit

and listen with a distant look
in your eyes; that they shimmer just beyond
your reaching — a reflection of a sun
    or some other source
    of light

whose capture is beyond your body's
limits. whose ownership
the contingencies of flesh won't allow.

fingernails

things must be going well,
everything's gotta be o.k.:
i looked at my hand today
and my fingernails
were all there.
i can stare at them now.
i don't know how
they grew. i never knew,
(realized), i'd stopped biting them.

ahem, ahem, i'll clear my throat.
this is bizarre, way too far-
fetched, i can catch
a glimpse of a manicured future.

this realization,
a complication —
something's (back, i'm under
attack.)
eating away at me. i'm
eating away at me.

the park

        perhaps some day, suddenly concerned
with numbers after $5.89 for two used books ($6.00, really,
because i won't have wanted change), i'll walk down
barrington street — and despite the aftermath of its sticky summe
rain, i'll read (alvarez's) *new poetry* and keep my thumb
under the cover. under the cover and cut off from the pages'
metastases — the metaphors, the language thick and hard, or soft
spreading — rich like butter, clogging and slowing us. and ignoring
my hand's ink-like smudge, yesterday's new acquaintance, i'll walk
to parks that i can't name and hope the paper, the bond
between the covers, will slip and slice and bleed the ink away
like simple summer rain or a mumbled, dreamed confession;
i'll notice statues, monuments, and the cemetery by the school
that dad went to; i'll stop to take a look.

        i'll say *hello* to dogs, but ignore their owners (and
that penmark oddity; my sickly thumb tattoo). and as i count
my steps, and the pages as i turn them, i'll entertain the fact
that a terminal exponent may well be a letter; that the variable
in this counting, this passage of days and weeks, the whole solutio
to this fatal mathematics, could be a literature of sorts; a syntax.

anthem

no, this great canadian novel doesn't open in
    the beginning of the month of november. and there
    are no faces, cold-scarred and dust-blinded
        by the winter's sweeping violence. no, instead

        i sing of the great asphalt plains.
        glistening hard and black, smooth and clean;
        save for the leaked rainbow-kaleidoscope swirls.

and the moon is just another streetlight, a slightly faded
    or obscured illumination — not a reasoning of tides, of
    the cresting waves that lament and steal husbands
        and fathers from their work. removed, it glows while

        i sing of the great asphalt plains.
        numbered neatly. divvied up for the new-age
        settlers. this, a new tundra below the tree line.

and only a suburb, (all sidewalk concrete and lawn ornament
    beautiful, all junior high school crush linear),
    greets the morning dawn. our not even close to log cabin
        dwelling has indoor plumbing, a central vac.

house league photo

this recollection is not a faded black-and-white
snapshot — i'm not old enough for that. coloured,
instead it is a commotion of smells and sounds, and
a straining to make out the shapes, the visual
components, through something akin to morning
breath-fog on hockey rink glass. in fact, the lapses,
the inaccuracies, are in themselves reminiscent

of a frustration not unlike the anxious zamboni
moments between the last lace or chin-strap and
the first cut of ice. and so this process of memory,
of revisiting ourselves, becomes that musty rubber
shuffle down the blade-scarred mat from locker-
room to cool motion. even these pictures,
their cardboard frames now just as ragtag as

our mismatched, ripped knee socks, are not
as concrete for me (though actually here
in hand) as the salt-sweat, leather-rot staleness
of the gear room, the smell of cold cigarette
smoke on my father's breath, or the dull thuds:
of pucks on the dead dashers
of boards, of early saturday morning trunks.

when skates break

    that ice in its liquid form is a solvent,
should not confuse matters. this is all about stains;
this game concerns itself with scars — in fact,

    the surgical violence of that first step
is merely a prelude, an introduction. a perverse
baptism. i remember our knees — carpet raw

    and bloody with tape-ball hockey
and too much sleep-over sugar; rec rooms alive
and stale gear crowded with the thrill of an oilers

    game on television out east. and especially
now, years later, after this afternoon's failure, when
the chill anticipation of this october night has shuddered

    and cracked, given way like we imagine
our childhood ponds never did — there is still
a sense of tired awe. and the broken, old goalie skates,

    a grade nine remnant now retired, are propped
in the corner — their blade acne, their cracked plastic,
become something more than nostalgia; become

    a grudging admission of the ambiguity of
physics and chemistry in the face of history. become
a memorial to the resiliency of water in all its states.

dressing-room religion

the zamboni's liquid absolution washed over
the night's early scars and imperfections, not unlike
a minor prophet's slow cup of river, or a mother's spittle-

moistened thumb. and then the bottom strap on
my right goalie pad gave way under my too eager
pre-game tugging; acquiesced to the child-like fervour

a two week lay-off and november's night cold
can produce. it should not have been such a surprise, given
that only moments before there had been a break, a snag

or disruption, in routine. and at that time my old
watch had re-appeared — jumped out from the bottom
of my gear bag after a year or so of salty hermitage. and

in that one snap of an instant, that moment of
leather's realization of its limits, even the easy give-and-take
of locker room banter seemed stilted, measured. time

became an issue, became concrete, became
a musty, sweat-soaked counting that clawed its way out of
a bag full of precautions and protections; showed itself

as resurgent, as lording over everything —
even the finest craftsmanship and tanning that northern
ontario could produce. so as i struggled with that

loose strip of leather, the rink airhorn's blast
immediacy suddenly ringing in my ears, i hoped the old rink
clock had blown a fuse or lost some bulbs. that

the scoreboard had ceased to function and we
would be left to ourselves; left to our temporary scratching
without the intrusion of counting and tabling of its results.

why football, sundays

there is the staccato report of cleats again
     meeting concrete at the edge
of steps and doorways. or the scabs of field caking
     elbows and cleat bottoms.
afterwards, the damp swell of jogging pants
     and their smack as they meet the bathroom
          floor's tile. and then

the slow ache that smothers and itches a finger, a
     wrist, an ankle.
the bruises swelling like polaroids from chill pink
     to the deeper maturity of
          the foreshadowing dirt
under nails still pinked with air; of a torn cuticle's
     red and a field's slick organic, mingling:
          the way they mix too well.

snow

(flurries
hurry) scurry
to

        their
places   on   the
    n
       a
k
    e
           d
asphaltasphaltasphaltasphaltcasphalt
             r
             a
             c
              k.

(frigid dandruff blitzkrieg),
that speckles
this

shadeofnewsprintskyline.

trees in ice

(with apologies to f. r. scott...)
loveliness
is a form—
(all) cruelty.

branching limbs snap
under
the weight of
falling mercury.

threshold

something peculiar, almost antithetical
occurs when in the midst
of flurries,

a child stoops,
takes a hand-
    full, and eats.

to take a bite, (no matter what
the colour, temperature,
or whose yard you're in)
is irrevocable. an act.

a change of state. a tongued interference.
a dry after-
        mouth.

when we eat snow
we accept a self, a story; we
consume what little is left
of that hazy space between waking
and sleep. this is the birth
of forgetting, and our lips are placenta wet.

winter airport mythology

wind and snow conspire here
   in a haphazard pageantry

   of weather — and the airport
parking lot is a temporary forgetting; a

blanketed reminder of the nature
   of imposed geographies, of

   the amnesias and missed lines
that mar our best-staged plans, our attempts

at civility. and despite the flowing
   stanza, the soliloquy that is

   our seeming mastery of the air —
the mystery of thermometers (a sort of

deus ex machina) intervenes and leaves
   only an inverse icarus, a lead

   or hero frozen by the lack of
a mark, by a growing white blindness.

newly

      metallic.
the colours of this belly lie —
make it seem simple, fair:
steel on steel.

but a newly gutted mackerel
is a contradiction. an inequation.

all sleek seashine
and blood.
a bellyache wave of redblack.

still moist and firm with sea, i run my hand along this —
cool belly smile,
hollow,
low tide.

this shell the sum of us,
        of our lost gills.

steaking halibut

he told me

    the first time he tried, he massacred it —
all ragged and uneven edges. years ago now, countless
    paychecks.

(just like my first 100 lb. of mackerel: poor fillets, 20 lb.
of fat in tubs, and the orange-gold roe long gone to garbage;
    further proof of my inadequacies.)

    first — the paper-towelling to remove what remains of
sea. then you cut the tail and bleed it. it's easier than you'd
    think —

just take the hose and run the water through until the crimson
fades. scrape the belly clean and rinse, and for god's sake

save the napes. make sure your blade is sharp. and
once you've started every inch or so you'll find a spot between

the vertebrae: there's no sense in going through bone. dulls a
    blade, and
an inch is a good thickness; grills up real nice.

    when you're traying them up be sure to separate the layers
with waxed paper: there's something in a halibut once sliced
    that turns it

if it's left to touch its own again.

voyeur

the background is almost as important
as the thing in the picture itself.
(of course i'm paraphrasing what a painter said.)

but look. through the window out
into the street. the sheet of
jaundiced light illuminates

two cars. indecent metal lovers, they steal
into each other. no shame as they come
recklessly together there at the corner.

but look again. beyond, behind: the trees,
just shades — woven, probing, reaching,
a bolt of grey cloth folding in on itself.

from the window, everything tangled and
fucking. and the flashing red stop light is overkill.

tectonics

    this afternoon the sidewalk asphalt
has shuddered and cracked, concentric and
web-like: a timed acquiescence.
                 we, too, acknowledge
certain fundamental shifts. i recall
last night's quaking — your half-turn
away and over — under a strata of duvet.
    in hindsight, this morning's newspaper
rustle, its grey-scale mapping
of the incident, was an aftershock; another
form of memory.
            and now i kick at the gravel
that edges this collapse and its stubborn refusal
of smoothness, of the settling qualities of time; i
imagine shattered plates strewn about, an
    aftermath.

a move to liquid

*there's a ceremony for everything, some take so long years can pass
before you realize how much has changed; even you are no longer
yourself.*

— *from "I Know Women" by Susan Goyette*

        there's a ceremony for everything
these days; i suppose there always has been — so
it should have come as no surprise that i sliced my hand
in the slick warmth of doing dishes one afternoon
in the days following your departure — a sort of ritual, a
bloodletting or a cleansing. it was under the strain of
the temperature's disparity; the cool shock of rinsing,
that the glass understood its hidden fissures all at once, and
cracked. and the fact that, in this instance, the breakage was
so quick, so immediate, is an intriguing one — given that

        some take so long. years can pass
in the breaking in some cases — with favourite mugs or
cups falling gradually into disrepair, slowly chipping away,
until they are eventually diminished so much that they
hardly resemble their former selves. it was to be expected, this
move to liquid—to blood, to water—given all the indiscriminate
reaching we do, the fumbling about in the murky pools of
our days; given that the movement is at once both quotidian
and filled with an undeniable danger — a possibility of violence:
of a misplaced steak knife, a plate chipped some indeterminate time

before. you realize how much has changed
only when, in reaching through the water, the former
crispness of it is missing. only when you notice, however slightly,
that some quality is gone, that the sink is no longer a stinging heat;
that it is instead a tepid jumble of unseen edges. and when this
fluid complacency takes hold, when it clings to and greases
your hands, your reaching — that is when the sudden ceremony
of shattered glass or some other domestic ritual is most
likely to occur. and really, considered for a moment, it does make
sense: that it would happen in this way, at this time when

even you are no longer yourself —
distracted or distanced from your actions, from your interaction
with all else; a time when your own comprehension of
the most simple things is a cloudy swirling, a sullied mixture, a
greying mess. it is in this dulled uncertainty of down-time,
of your submersion in the everyday, that the sudden pain will
surface; will appear and announce itself in a sort of liquid
language — a baptismal wound that in its stinging flow serves
to remind you that there is still in you, at any given moment, a
keen ability to feel; the possibility of unexpected change.

apostrophe: a mess of floor
   — after a photograph by M. van Dam

        this is the door as object, not utility. not as the oaken modesty
    of a boy
in some crowded farmhouse near saint john years ago, not as the studied
    instrument of just how
drunk or angry or both he was as he left or arrived. no, this is the door
    as simply fallen. it is
hardwood, or seems from this distance to be, and lies on the floor. the
    paint is a greying and

    ruddy white; is chipping all around. near the top there is a
    suggestion of nails, long
since removed and almost forgotten; of a place to hang coats, keys, or a
    jacket; of a picture or trinket,
perhaps. the darkened floorboards beneath, speckled as they are with an
    antiquing of paint and
crumbled drywall, run perpendicular to the door's grain, though they are
    not at cross-purposes.

    this is not the door as countless hours — the cutting, planing,
    sanding, painting, and all
the rest. this is the door as something old and used up, fallen over; as
    finished with responsibilities and
simply ready for the floor. it seems at home there in the damp, the dust
    — what is left. this is the door
as apology, as a way of letting go. there is nothing to be gained from a
    consideration of the frame.

snow; a fear of dying

The plan is the body.
The plan is the body.
The plan is the body.

> *— from "The Plan Is the Body" by Robert Creeley*

the plan is the body —
is in the physicality of all this as i glance out
the window. and there, the november light is
in its solid form — frozen, pieced and chopped —
falling from the trees like ticker-tape. announcing
victories and deaths, conclusions of all sorts. and
the wind outside is moderately strong: it can be
heard, and it can be seen in the nervous postures
of birch and spruce. and this snow, it is
a smart suggestion, really, of what

the plan is. the body
knows that familiar swirling towards a destination, down.
and i am certain there was something like it swirling
in my mother's blood, in my grandfather's veins — something
snow-pale and rare, and not quite right; some thing
that seemed to come and go, but was truly weather constant.
and that blood certainty is mine — an arterial legacy, a
flowing probability of days, weeks and years. it is a cool
flow, this icy thickening that racks and scrapes and slows
me from the inside; it is hidden proof of

the plan. is the body
that much a diagram, a window-framed picture, a
second-hand mapping or charting? on days like these
it would seem to be, so now i am obsessed with nature —
with its understated tallies: blood's snow and its piling
virus-frantic. i am concerned with ideas of pressures and
systems, with the way seasons bleed into each other
like colours, and the fact that drifts melt to newly grown
green; that even here we always return, however
briefly, to crumbling earth and fields, and stones.

winter felt

the coming of winter has announced itself today; has taken
    the form of an itch of peacoat felt that bothers my arm
    here as i walk this snow crunch gravel. and this

path: all along this arboreal midway each tree is selling itself
    — a painted, suburban whore anxious for attention or
    some sort of affirmation, something before the last

snap cold. and there is a familiar danger to all this — to these
    autumnal sways of oak or maple as they court and
    coax the sizzling violence of power lines; to

the drunken slouch of leaves shifting slightly, as if to remind us
    of the uneasiness of sleep, of rest. so as the wind
    suggests itself to the fading limbs around me i can

already smell the mould, the stale chemistry of decay and
    endings. the scent of departure, of leaves moistly
    struggling against the process of forgetting themselves.

five
other dissociative disorders

morning, laundry

    the fact that i have again not properly made
my bed introduces itself as a tangle of duvet, a pressure
on my chest as i lie prone; as a wrinkle of sheets that patterns
my elbow like sleeping in grass in july. and here in the sheen

    of morning through windows, shadow and some other
of night's composite parts are soaked into them, the sheets,
like a thinned paint; like a varnish or an antiquing — a recognition
of aging, or at least some other, less formalized process. our sheets

    are a reluctant mapping of last night; are the remainder
of most everything this venetian blind dawn has erased. to
the left of my shoulder there is a bit of life left on the burgundy
linen: white, dry and cracked, like old school glue or forgotten

    semen. the only hair on the pillow is mine. later, in
the impersonal grey of the laundry, the industrial rumble and
whirr of the rinse-and-spin cycle is a critical theory, a re-thinking,
a new historicism. the iron is an amnesia — a steamy forgetting haze.

a child's toy, in the grass

A blue against the easy clarities of sky,
a blue that eats the light, a bruise

— from "Kinds of Blue #76 (Evening Snow)" by Don MacKay

    a blue. (against the easy clarities of sky —
those straightforward tones of midday — it is
still, despite all its possible associative complexity,
a colour.) and in fact, from a distance, regarded
less than intently, that is perhaps all it is
— a shade; a slight remembrance become
physical. and so the plastic ring, a misplaced
part of a child's fisher price stacking toy,
is found. found and, through the low swirling
heat of this summer day and its airy illusion
of melting, lost again to its visual essence;
to blue. to a category of sorts, a shared
existence with robin's eggs, certain flowers, or
other blue things in grass. but this is actually

    a blue that eats. the light — a bruise —
reflected, is evidence of it, is proof that this
childhood relic is a dangerous, deep blue. and
this discovery — it is a sullen pooling of
the summer's light that, collected, sits stagnant
and somewhat removed; pre-occupied. the plastic,
now taken out of its surroundings, is like
memory in its oddest forms: the ones that force
us to question even our own most dearly held

facts. it is as if we had seen this toy before, as if this was not discovery, but recollection, and this moment a sort of deja vu. the entire instant and its elements — grass, plastic, all — simply reminders of breakdowns, of half-lives.

i imagine middle age; paint with my hands

— the small, brown, unlocked luggage
that's completed its work in this world.

—from "Suitcase Song" by Albert Goldbarth

the small, brown, unlocked luggage
of the plot (that has, for the moment,
stopped its wormy tumbling at the edge
of this backyard garden — clotted briefly,
like the urgent seething tangle of passengers
leaving a railcar at the end of the broken
concrete platform at the end of a long, dry
voyage) is intriguing. it begs questions with
its haphazard spilling and clumping. it seems,
at first glance, used up — like something

that's completed its work in this world —
like the shade of brown that results, when, as
a child, one mixed all the paints together
in an attempt at creation. and now my hands
are still, years later, filthy. soiled not with
an experimental innocence, but instead with
the dogged clawing of years. i have convinced
myself i need to plant, to nurture something,
before (for all the earth, concrete, and drying
skin) i can no longer distinguish my hands.

localization of memory

broadly speaking, theories of memory can be divided
into theories focussing on events at the molecular level
and theories that emphasize changes in large clusters or ensembles.

that the milk was left out last night reveals itself
as this morning string of pearls, this added valuation
of my coffee. there are books on the floor open

to pages. if the sun were out this morning it would surely
surprise me, would certainly redefine the colour yellow in
complicity with the paint on these walls. both the sour brown

waking of my mug and the early evening mint of routine
today remind me of you, or of the idea of you. there is no one
in the shower. the door closes quietly behind me. walking

this wet morning, traffic sizzles like the breakfast grill
of some all-night diner; the asphalt is a used-up black — fat
and slick with the scrap and trimming lesions of last night

congealing to the side. the four-way stop, an aphasia, clots
and falters momentarily — a stutter of rote morning. it regains
its composure, and somewhere a light turns red, turns green.

a consequence of liquor

But full and dark with the promise of that fullness,
That time when one can no longer wander away

 —*from "As One Put Drunk into the Packet-Boat" by John Ashber*

but full and dark with the promise of that fullness
still — although now only in some sort of jumbled,
clumsy, allusive way — the various states of the bottle
are resigned to a momentary, wet stillness. and the sudden
tip of my elbow is still tinged with that instant of glass's
forced stumble, its conclusion. i have smacked my beer
drunkenly, elbowed it to the floor. so in this smoky
haze, faced with this change in circumstance, i am unsteady
both with liquor and a knowledge of the unpredictability
of endings in a number of senses: of an ale or of a lager, of

that time.   when one can no longer wander away
for fear of stepping on the possible wreckage — the sepia
cullet of some celebration — and in doing so crushing both i
and any chance of its memory, a sort of time has ended. a
period or era has been completed. and what is left, more
often than not, is a sort of painful recollection — disordered
and incomplete — of what may or may not have been. what
is left, once the table has been upset and all the bottles left
seeping or broken, is a mess of dangerous edges stewing in
their contents, everything the browning shade of old photos.

what we sometimes mistake as love: the right hand of a pioneer radiologist, 1932

it does not seem, on first inspection of the two
black and white diagrams provided, human at all. if challenged,
or confronted with a wager, you would guess it more

reptilian, possibly avian, and certainly primitive
in origin — rugged and concerned with utility, like old boots,
familiar with use as a worn saddlebag. but it is, if nothing

else, beautiful, in that it is a consequence of a sort of passion
— of what we sometimes mistake as love. the sketches, whatever
their inadequacies or shortcomings, make one thing

clear: there are two fingers reaching, claw-like, hawkish, and
a weathered thumb intact. and this hand, it is a cruel
and unmistakable artifact: a token of remembrance for something

elusive as atoms and haphazard as their collisions and
distortions. it is a kind of counting to three — the fingers:
your parents' tired warnings become car accident-physical and

photographically immediate. it also, perhaps, holds a clue: one
that reveals through missing digits and in all its disfigured
fleshing out, that whatever this one man reached for, however

figuratively, it grasped back; grasped back and held him
dearly, tightly. that it held, that it consumed him — indeed,
too much so. and as for the amputation: it must have

been, given its circumstantial surroundings, an event spotted
and mottled with mixed emotions. just imagine for a moment
the possible pang of losing an unwanted child — imagine

the aftermath and odd-shaped attempts at normalcy;
the undertakings constantly shaded with shadow pains, with finge
lurking just beyond the capabilities of film, of the visual. of

even the execution of one's grip on a morning's coffee cup —
that simple task — serving as constant reminder. it does not seem
on further inspection, given these explanations, human at all.

a death of neurons

    prone, at rug level, they
catch
my eye. clippings. and it occurs:
our bodies will interpret,

historicize us. in the bone certainty
of these,

    our living remains, our
snake's skin we shed as we see fit, there is no denial.
there is no denial of lovers, their

                 hair or skin a stolen
moment become physical, once we catalogue them
here, even if the heart has long since washed

its hands of them. there is no fiction in
the blood remnants of scab, or bits
of earth — catalogued injuries, both —

that gather and insinuate.
a ragged toothiness of edges is
an automatic writing, a psychological investigation.

the jaundiced index accusations persist, know
more of us after they have been
              discarded, ash-tumbled to the floor.

the hagiography of photographs

just know they aren't to be trusted, regardless
    of a grandmother's weighty antique insistence —
    the false sense of loyalty a cookie can produce.

even as a child i always held those collections, despite
    their grey-scale certainty of tints and colourations; of
    accurate representations, suspect. and so, no matter

how crowded, how gaudy the frames, how well dusted
    the assortment, i have been wary. just know it is
    a familial jargon, a blood hieroglyphics. this picture

campaign is a limited vocabulary, a cut and paste poetry
    of fridge magnet proportions, an abridged dime store
    dictionary conversation; all polite — these gatherings

on the living room maple or oak. you'll see dust velours
    the glass — a reminder, a convenient marriage of what
    it is we end up as. the frames don't break themselves, all

early morning whisky frantic. just know that the look
    of years' jaundice on a snapshot and the sickly cheek bloom
    of bruise are both yellows — similar but not the same.

an idea of morning

It is like a thing of ether that exists
Almost as predicate. But it exists,
It exists, it is visible, it is, it is.

> *— from "The Auroras of Autumn" by Wallace Stevens*

it is like a thing of ether that exists
only in theory, only in terms of certain
senses. and in the tenuous space between
that of waking and that of dream, there
is its kind of snowy energy; one that dissipates
as soon as it is grasped. so the morning is
a brief type of sadness; it relates to dream

almost as predicate. but it exists
nonetheless — though only for mere moments
in its purest form. and in the gleaming
aftermath, the bright instants when, for all intents
and purposes, we forget it — lost in the later
process of our dreams' transformation into
memory — we should still not deny that

it exists. it is visible, it is — it is
the eyelids' transition from deep black to
orange-red. and this stage of waking, this
morning, is not a discrete event, but instead
a process — a frantic counting of
the fissile splits of seconds between the urge
to stir and the opening of the eyes.

Notes on the poems

The definitions that head the individual sections of "notes towards a garden glossary" are taken from *The President's Choice Garden Guide Series: Garden Remedies* (Alpha Corporation/Susan Yates, Publisher, 1999).

The poems in the section entitled "scleroderma" deal both directly and indirectly with my mother's lengthy illness and eventual death. They are for her.

The first, italicized stanza of "localization of memory" is from Aman U. Khan's *Clinical Disorders of Memory* (Plenum Publishing Corporation, 1986).

The first lines of each stanza in "drifting" are from Michael Ondaatje's "To A Sad Daughter".